LEWIS LATIMER

A BRILLIANT INVENTOR

By Janel Rodríguez

Illustrated by Subi Bosa

Children's Press®
An imprint of Scholastic Inc.

**LEWIS LATIMER
HOUSE MUSEUM**

Special thanks to our consultant Hugh Price and to the staff at the Lewis Latimer House Museum in Queens. This book would not have been possible without them. The activity on pages 34 and 35 is based on the STEAM projects and lesson plans offered by the museum at: LewisLatimerHouse.org/educators

Special thanks to our consultant Dr. Le'Trice Donaldson, assistant professor of history at Texas A&M University-Corpus Christi, for making sure the text of the book is authentic and historically accurate.

Thank you to Chad Shapiro for his insight into the history of the light bulb.

Library of Congress Cataloging-in-Publication Data
Names: Rodríguez, Janel, author.
Title: Lewis Latimer: A brilliant inventor / by Janel Rodríguez.
Description: First edition. | New York, NY: Children's Press, an imprint of Scholastic Inc., 2023. | Series: Bright minds | Includes bibliographical references and index. | Audience: Ages 8–10. | Audience: Grades 4–6. | Summary: "A biography series highlighting the work and social impact of BIPOC inventors"—Provided by publisher.
Identifiers: LCCN 2022028715 (print) | LCCN 2022028716 (ebook) | ISBN 9781338864175 (library binding) | ISBN 9781338864182 (paperback) | ISBN 9781338864199 (ebk)
Subjects: LCSH: Latimer, Lewis Howard, 1848–1928—Juvenile literature. | African American inventors—Biography—Juvenile literature. | Light bulbs—History—Juvenile literature. | BISAC: JUVENILE NONFICTION / Biography & Autobiography / General | JUVENILE NONFICTION / Technology / Inventions | LCGFT: Biographies.
Classification: LCC T40.L37 R63 2023 (print) | LCC T40.L37 (ebook) | DDC 621.32/6092 [B]—dc23/eng/20220711
LC record available at https://lccn.loc.gov/2022028715
LC ebook record available at https://lccn.loc.gov/2022028716

10 9 8 7 6 5 4 3 2 1   23 24 25 26 27

Printed in China   62
First edition, 2023

Book design by Kathleen Petelinsek
Book prototype design by Maria Bergós / Book&Look

Photos ©: cover top right, cover bottom right: United States Patent and Trademark Office; 5 center: Science History Images/Alamy Images; 6 map: Elisa Lara/Dreamstime; 7 top right: The Granger Collection; 8 bottom left: Pictorial Press Ltd/Alamy Images; 9 top right: Courtesy of the Ohio History Connection (AL03045); 9 center: Courtesy of the Massachusetts Historical Society; 10 bottom: Culture Club/Getty Images; 11 top left: Alexander Gardner/Library of Congress; 12 center: Everett/Shutterstock; 13 top: Courtesy of Louis H. Smaus/Navy.mil; 13 bottom: William Morris Smith/Library of Congress; 14 top: Courtesy of the Massachusetts Historical Society; 16 bottom right: United States Patent and Trademark Office; 17 top right: Sheila Terry/Science Source; 17 bottom right: United States Patent and Trademark Office; 18 top right: Courtesy of the Chad Shapiro Collection; 19 bottom left, 19 bottom right: United States Patent and Trademark Office; 20 center left: Science History Images/Alamy Images; 20 center: Science History Images/Alamy Images; 20 center right, 20 bottom: Historia/Shutterstock; 23 center left, 23 bottom right: Randy Duchaine/Alamy Images; 24 center left: New York Public Library; 24 center right: United States Patent and Trademark Office; 25 top right: United States Patent and Trademark Office; 25 bottom left: Randy Duchaine/Alamy Images; 26 center: Elliott Jerome Brown Jr.; 27 center right: Science Source; 29 top right: Randy Duchaine/Alamy Images; 30 center left: Robert K. Chin/Storefronts/Alamy Images; 30 center right: Photo by Lydie Raschka for InsideSchools, a project of the Center for New York City Affairs at The New School; 30 bottom: Ned Gerard/Hearst Connecticut Media/AP Images; 32 center: Manuscripts, Archives and Rare Books Division, Schomburg Center for Research in Black Culture/The New York Public Library; 33 top: Courtesy of the Chad Shapiro Collection; 34 center: cswngd/Flickr; 40: Author Self Portrait by Janel Rodriguez.

All other photos © Designed by Freepik and Shutterstock.

TABLE OF CONTENTS

LET'S SHINE A LIGHT ON...

Have you ever noticed how in cartoons a light bulb appears over a character's head when they have an idea? Or how the word "brilliant" is often used to describe a smart person?

...LEWIS LATIMER

Lewis Latimer was like a light bulb. He was brilliant, and he helped people see things more clearly, too. His work with the light bulb and with **electricity** improved the lives of people all over the world.

I shine with ideas!

To learn more about how he did that, let's turn the spotlight on the life of Lewis Latimer.

HIGHLIGHTS OF A LIFE

Lewis Howard Latimer was born on September 4, 1848, in **Chelsea, Massachusetts**.

He married **Mary Wilson Lewis** on November 15, 1873.

They had two children: **Emma Jeanette** and **Louise Rebecca**.

He died on December 11, 1928, in **Queens, New York**.

DO THE MATH!
1928 − 1848 = 80
Lewis Latimer lived to be eighty years old!

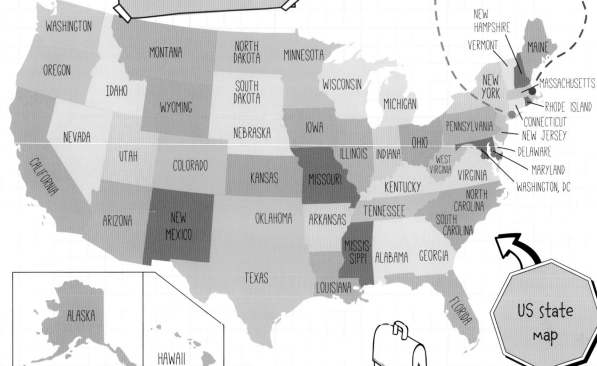

US state map

KNOWN FOR...

- ✅ His **drafting** and drawing ability

- ✅ Being an inventor

- ✅ Helping develop the **patent** for the first telephone

- ✅ Working on the development of the electric light bulb

- ✅ Being the only Black member of "Edison Pioneers"

- ✅ His intelligence

- ✅ Being a good family man and a civil rights advocate

> We create our future by well improving present opportunities.

As Lewis's words show, he believed in "improvement." This means he was always looking for ways to learn more and make things better for himself and everyone else.

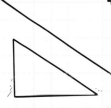

★ A GREAT ESCAPE

In 1842, Lewis's parents, George and Rebecca, were an **enslaved** couple being forced to live on a **plantation** in Virginia. When Rebecca was going to have a baby, they decided to escape to Boston, Massachusetts. They did not want their children to be enslaved, too.

Let's hide in that ship!

WHY THEY RAN

For nearly 250 years, Black people had been enslaved in America. They were bought and sold and treated as property. Many were taken to plantations in the South of the United States. There, for generations, they were forced to work without pay. Many were whipped by their cruel owners. Their rights as **citizens**, or even as human beings, were not recognized. It was a terrible way to live. In Northern states, like Massachusetts, **slavery** was phasing out. That was where George and Rebecca were headed.

But after they made it to Boston, George was caught, arrested, and brought to trial. He was **defended** by William Lloyd Garrison, an important **abolitionist** (a person who fought to **abolish**—or end—slavery), and **Frederick Douglass**, a well-known Black **activist**. George's case became famous all around the country. In the end, Douglass helped raise money to buy George's freedom. George was free!

A DREADFUL DECISION

For a while, life was good. **George** and Rebecca had three more children. George attended antislavery rallies with Douglass, and he became a hero to abolitionists. *The Latimer Journal,* an abolitionist newspaper, was started in his honor. Some admirers called him Latimer the Lion.

THE LATIMER JOURNAL, AND NORTH STAR.

All my children have been born free.

But some years later, in 1857, an enslaved man named Dred Scott lost his court battle for freedom.

Perhaps afraid that he could lose his freedom, too, George disappeared without a trace.

GROWING PAINS

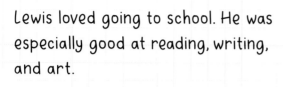

Lewis loved going to school. He was especially good at reading, writing, and art.

But his family needed money. So by the time he was ten, Lewis had to leave school to go to work instead. Among other jobs, he ran errands for a law office.

Little did Lewis know, war was on the horizon.

Railroads that linked the states together would soon be built. They made traveling much easier.

CHANGE IN THE AIR

As Lewis grew, so did the country around him. In particular, the northern United States were **expanding** through industry. Many factories and railroads were being built. The general understanding that slavery is wrong was also growing.

The South wanted to keep enslaving people—in fact, they wanted to have even *more* enslaved people. Plantation owners argued that this would increase the number of crops they could grow. This caused tensions to rise between the North and the South.

THIS MEANS WAR

Abraham Lincoln was against expanding slavery. When he was elected president, the Southern states began to **secede** (withdraw) from the United States and form their own country, which they called the **Confederate** States of America.

The North, called the Union, did not want the country to be divided. They did not want to go to war. But on April 12, 1861, when the Confederate army attacked the Union army post at **Fort** Sumter in South Carolina, Union forces fought back. This officially started the Civil War.

Abraham Lincoln was the sixteenth president of the United States of America.

The states that belonged to the Union (seen here in blue, like the color of their uniforms) were antislavery.

The states that belonged to the **Confederacy** (seen here in gray, like the color of their uniforms) were proslavery.

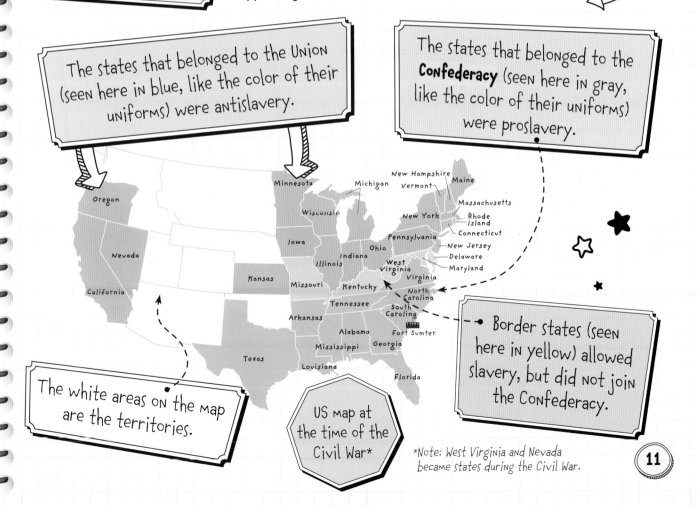

Border states (seen here in yellow) allowed slavery, but did not join the Confederacy.

The white areas on the map are the territories.

US map at the time of the Civil War*

*Note: West Virginia and Nevada became states during the Civil War.

11

LANDSMAN AT SEA

Men had to be at least eighteen years old to fight in the war. Lewis was only fifteen, but he still wanted to defend the Union. This is why he lied about his age and joined the Navy as a landsman.

WHAT WAS A LANDSMAN?
A landsman was the lowest rank in the Navy at the time. It was usually given to new recruits who had more land experience than sea experience. However, once a landsman had served at sea for a year, he could be called a seaman.

Lewis would have looked something like this in his Navy uniform. Notice how the unidentified sailor in this photo looks underage, like Lewis was!

Lewis served on a Union gunboat called the USS *Massasoit*. While on the boat, Lewis spent time on the James River in Virginia. This was near the plantations where his parents had been enslaved.

The *Massasoit* was a wooden steamboat. It was converted into a gunboat for the war.

The Civil War ended on April 9, 1865, when Confederate General Robert E. Lee surrendered to Union General Ulysses S. Grant after a battle in Appomattox County, Virginia. There Grant surrounded Lee's troops with an army that included 5,000 Black soldiers.

By the end of the Civil War, about 19,000 Black sailors served in the Union navy and 179,000 Black soldiers served in the Union army.

A group of Black Union soldiers poses with their musical instruments.

TURNING POINT

After the war, seventeen-year-old Lewis began working for a patent office called Crosby & Gould in Boston.

The Crosby & Gould office was above the Boston Five Cents Savings Bank.

WHAT'S A PATENT?

A patent is a legal document. It gives an inventor the sole rights to manufacture or sell their own invention. In order to be awarded, a patent must be unique. Patents often include **mechanical drawings**.

In a patent office, artists called draftsmen help inventors by making mechanical drawings of their inventions. These drawings have all the parts of the invention clearly labeled. They also include instructions on how the invention should work.

If you want to see two examples of mechanical drawings, turn to pages 16 and 17.

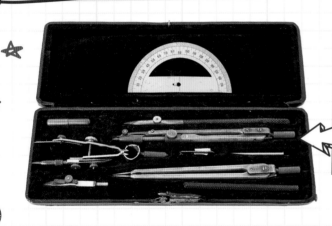

Draftsmen needed to use a special set of drawing tools, such as this one. This is a set Lewis bought for himself.

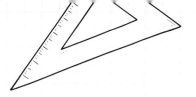

After watching the draftsmen drawing, Lewis thought, "I can do that!" He began buying the art supplies he needed in order to practice mechanical drawing at home.

When Lewis thought he was finally ready, he asked a draftsman:

Can I draw for you?

YOU draw for ME? Ha ha ha! This I gotta see!

Lewis impressed the boss, who promoted him to the position of draftsman. In time, Lewis went from working alongside other draftsmen to becoming lead draftsman. His salary was raised from three dollars a week to twenty!

Well! Whaddya know? He's good!

HIS FIRST INVENTION

Drafting mechanical drawings for other people's patents excited Lewis so much that he began to think like an inventor, too. Wherever he went, he started seeing things that could use improvement. That's how an inventor thinks: "How do I make things better for others?"

There's room for improvement here!

In 1874, he and a man named Charles W. Brown did just that. Together, they redesigned the "water closet" that was used on railroad cars.

The patent looked like this when they submitted it. This is Lewis's real drawing!

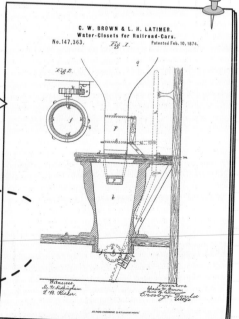

C. W. BROWN & L. H. LATIMER.
Water-Closets for Railroad-Cars.
No. 147,363. Patented Feb. 10, 1874.

Specially designed for a moving train!

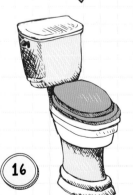

Water closet = a toilet

HELPING HISTORY

In 1876, a teacher asked Lewis for help. He had an invention he needed to patent as soon as possible. And he wanted Lewis to make the drawings for it.

Lewis agreed to help. But it meant working quickly and long into the night. When at last he was done, the teacher submitted the patent just in time to beat a similar application that a different inventor would submit a few hours later.

Whew! That was close!

Thanks to Lewis, the teacher, **Alexander Graham Bell**, won the patent and became known worldwide as the inventor of the telephone. What a special and important invention! And Lewis helped make it happen!

Here is a copy of one of the detailed drawings Lewis likely drew carefully for Bell.

A BRIGHT IDEA

In 1880, Lewis moved with his family to Bridgeport, Connecticut. There he began working at the US Electric Lighting Company as an assistant manager and drafter. His boss, Hiram Maxim, was an inventor whose biggest competitor was Thomas Alva Edison.

Thomas Edison in 1879

WHO WAS THOMAS ALVA EDISON?

He was the brains behind many important inventions of the late 1800s and early 1900s. For years, he and other scientists around the world had been working on versions of the "**electric lamp**." But on January 27, 1880, he won the historic US patent for what is considered the first **incandescent lamp** for home use. (Edison dreamed of a future where light bulbs replaced candles and oil lamps!) There was only one problem: His light bulb did not stay lit for very long. It needed a better **filament**.

➤ This is what the light bulb was called at the time.

This was another way to refer to the light bulb at the time.

Working filament

Broken filament

WHAT IS A FILAMENT?

A filament is the wire or fiber inside the bulb itself that glows when electricity passes through it. Lead wires connect it to the rest of the light bulb.

A RACE AROUND THE WORLD

Scientists around the globe raced to discover a better filament. They wanted to "reinvent" the light bulb and gain fame and riches.

Maxim wanted to claim that victory for himself. He had Lewis working around the clock. But in July 1880, Edison won again when he found that a filament made of **carbonized** bamboo could keep a bulb shining for fifty days straight.

Still, Lewis did not give up. He was always looking for ways to make things better! Shortly after Edison's patent, Lewis filed two patents. They were both meant to improve the light bulb.

The first one improved the connection between the **carbon** filament and the lead wires. He did this by flattening the ends of the wires and covering them in copper. Even if it was never put into commercial use, this patent was meant to make light bulbs more durable and energy efficient.

The second one created a faster and easier way to make carbonized filaments. This patent was put to use by Maxim between 1882 and 1884. It made light bulbs more affordable and longer-lasting.

(No Model) J. V. NICHOLS & L. H. LATIMER.
ELECTRIC LAMP.
No. 247,097.   Patented Sept. 13, 1881.

Fig. 1.   Fig. 2.   Fig. 3.

Witnesses.

Inventors.

With these two patents, Lewis made history as the first Black inventor to contribute to the development of the light bulb.

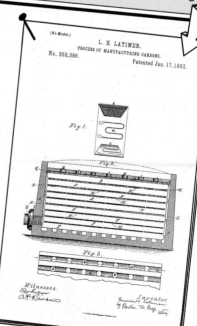

(No Model)
L. H. LATIMER.
PROCESS OF MANUFACTURING CARBONS.
No. 252,386.   Patented Jan. 17, 1882.

Fig. 1.

Fig. 2.

Fig. 3.

Witnesses.

Inventor.

CITIES OF LIGHT

Lewis learned a lot about electricity. He became an expert in the new technology. Maxim recognized this, and he made Lewis chief superintendent of the incandescent lighting department. Maxim placed Lewis in charge of forty white men. This was a very unusual position for a Black man at that time!

We need to update our lighting systems!
You need Latimer!
New York City

And when leaders in cities like New York, Philadelphia, and Montreal asked Maxim to help them set up their first electricity systems, **Maxim** knew exactly who to send to them.

But we need to set up power plants!
Latimer can do it!
And lay down electric wiring!
That would be Latimer!
Philadelphia
And connect them to street lamps!
Latimer's your man!
Montreal

IN HOT WATER

Maxim sent Lewis to all these cities. At each stop, Lewis trained groups of men to be electricians and taught them how to wire their cities for power.

Maxim next sent Lewis to London, England, to help set up an incandescent lamp department at his company there. But once he arrived, Lewis was treated badly by the other employees. They clearly did not want a Black man telling them what to do.

It was some of the worst racial **discrimination** Lewis experienced in his life.

Lewis was an electrifying presence wherever he went!

In London, I was in hot water from the day I came until I returned.

LONDON

Of his time in London, Lewis wrote this in his diary. He was very glad to return home to the United States.

THE GREAT DEFENDER

In 1882, Lewis found himself in his home country but without a job. Maxim had quit the electricity business and decided to stay in England.

In time, Lewis found work with the Edison Electric Light Company in New York City (yes, the company owned by Maxim's former **rival**, Thomas Edison!). This work sometimes required him to defend Edison's patents in a court of law. Because of his patent experience, Lewis did this really well. He was key in winning many cases, and he earned the respect of those who saw him in action.

Lewis taught himself French while in Canada, and he learned German as well. His knowledge of other languages became very useful when he defended Edison's patents against international challengers.

Le brevet appartient à Edison.

This means "The patent belongs to Edison" in French.

Das Patent gehört Edison.

This means "The patent belongs to Edison" in German.

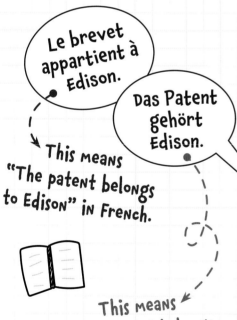

A PIONEER IN THE FIELD

Edison was always on the lookout for sharp minds. However, he most often hired white men. In 1918, top aides in Edison's company were assembled into a special group called Edison Pioneers.

Lewis Latimer was not white. But because he had a bright mind and was a prized employee, he was one of the first official members of the group.

This is the certificate inducting Lewis Latimer into Edison Pioneers.

This photograph of Edison Pioneers was taken in 1918, the year the group was established.

An older Lewis Latimer is in the front.

UPLIFTING INVENTIONS

Lewis never stopped thinking about ways to improve the world around him.

In 1886, he patented an invention he called an "**apparatus** for cooling and disinfecting." It was a sort of early air conditioner and air filter in one.

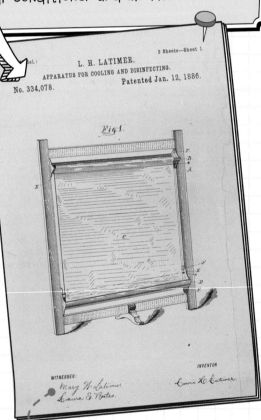

(No Model.)

L. H. LATIMER.
APPARATUS FOR COOLING AND DISINFECTING.

No. 334,078.   Patented Jan. 12, 1886.

2 Sheets—Sheet 1.

Fig. 1.

WITNESSES:
Mary W. Latimer
Laura S. Yates.

INVENTOR
Lewis H. Latimer

In this patent, Lewis's wife, Mary, is listed as a **witness** of this invention. You can see her name here.

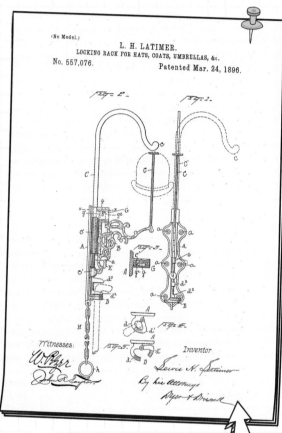

(No Model.)

L. H. LATIMER.
LOCKING RACK FOR HATS, COATS, UMBRELLAS, &c.

No. 557,076.   Patented Mar. 24, 1896.

Witnesses:
W. Pfizer

Inventor
Lewis N. Latimer
By his Attorneys
Dyer & Driscoll

In 1896, Lewis submitted a patent for a wall rack designed to hold hats, coats, and umbrellas. It could be extended and spread across a wall. It was later used in restaurants, hotels, and office buildings.

Lewis loved to read and research, so books were very important to him. But traditional bookends cannot always keep books from toppling over.

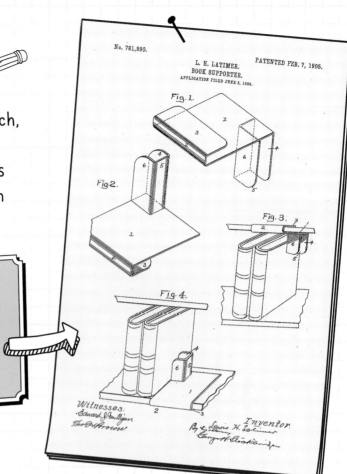

In 1905, he created this "book supporter" to keep books securely standing in a row on a desktop.

INCANDESCENT
ELECTRIC LIGHTING.

A Practical Description of the Edison System.

BY
L. H. LATIMER.

TO WHICH IS ADDED THE
DESIGN AND OPERATION OF INCANDESCENT STATIONS.

By C. J. FIELD.

AND A PAPER ON
THE MAXIMUM EFFICIENCY OF INCANDESCENT LAMPS.

By JOHN W. HOWELL.

NEW YORK:
D. VAN NOSTRAND COMPANY,
23 MURRAY AND 27 WARREN STREET.
1890.

Lewis also wrote a book called Incandescent Electric Lighting: A Practical Description of the Edison System. It was published in 1890. It was the first book ever published on electric lighting by a Black writer. It must have fit neatly in the book supporter!

LOVE OF THE ARTS

Work kept Lewis very busy! He used his talents for inventing, drafting, practicing patent law, **electrical engineering**, and for learning languages. But even when he wasn't working, he kept busy, too. He had an active social life, played the flute and other musical instruments, wrote poetry, and continued to paint.

This is a portrait Lewis painted of one of his daughters.

He wrote stories and poems that were published in magazines. An editor of one magazine once wrote: "Lewis, poetry is your 'forte.'" ("Forte" means "specialty.") He thought the poems were amazing!

In 1902, Lewis wrote a play called *Comedy*. He was paid more than **seventy-five dollars** for it and saw it performed on a Brooklyn stage.

→ This is about 2,600 dollars today.

Beginning in the late nineteenth century, a new invention called the kinetophone allowed people to watch movies on a small screen built into a cabinet. It also had sound, which came through earphones. (Do you see them in the photo?)

Wow!

In 1913, when Lewis was sixty-five years old, he wrote another play that he tried to get made into a movie by Edison's motion picture studio. Sadly, it was never produced, and the studio, which produced hundreds of short movies a year, closed in 1918.

A GREAT LIGHT IS DIMMED

In his later years, Lewis worked as a patent consultant. He also did volunteer work. It included teaching draftsmanship, engineering, and English to **immigrants** for a charitable organization in Manhattan.

In 1922, when his eyesight began to fail, Lewis was forced to retire. And when his wife died in 1924, his overall health began to decline, too. Wanting to boost his spirits, Lewis's daughters had a collection of his poems printed in a book for his seventy-seventh birthday.

On December 11, 1928, Lewis Latimer died in Queens, New York. He was eighty years old. Edison Pioneers announced his death and paid tribute with an **obituary**. It said:

Broadmindedness, **versatility** in the accomplishment of things **intellectual** and **cultural,** a **linguist,** a devoted husband and father, all were characteristic of him, and his **genial** presence will be missed from our gatherings.

broadmindedness: an understanding and acceptance of various points of view

cultural: with an appreciation for the arts, such as music, literature, and painting

versatility: ability to do many things and adapt to many situations

linguist: someone who can speak different languages

intellectual: involving thought and reason

genial: warm and friendly

LEGACY

These days, more and more people are learning about the life and legacy of Lewis Latimer.

His former home in Queens, New York, has been turned into the Lewis Latimer House Museum. It has a permanent exhibit and is open to visitors.

When Lewis's home was in danger of being demolished, it was moved from Holly Avenue in Flushing to 137th Street, also in Flushing, where it stands today.

P.S. 56 Lewis H. Latimer

There is a public **school** in Brooklyn, New York, that is named after him.

And there is a statue of him in Bridgeport, Connecticut.

Erected in 2015, the statue depicts Lewis holding a light bulb, the invention he was constantly improving while he worked for Hiram Maxim.

He has even popped up in the movies. For instance, in the 2017 movie *The Current War* (starring Benedict Cumberbatch as Thomas Edison), Lewis Latimer is an actual character in the film, portrayed by the actor Simon Manyonda.

Actor Simon Manyonda as Lewis Latimer

It looks like Lewis got into motion pictures after all!

WELL DONE!

Lewis drew this **portrait** of himself in 1913. It looks much like a drawing for a patent.

Notice, too, that he didn't draw his face. Instead, we see his whole body, but mostly from the back. And he has made himself small—dwarfed by his mechanical pencil!

This suggests that he didn't see himself as important. Rather, he saw what he could do for others as important.

He was a humble man.

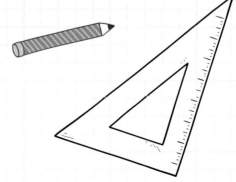

This is a **poem** Lewis wrote for Thomas Edison's seventy-second birthday. It was meant to honor a well-lived life.

When we read it now, we can see how it can also describe the life of Lewis: It was, as the last line reads, "Well done."

-- February 11, 1919 --

by

L. H. LATIMER.

Once more we meet to eat fried carp,
Or other fish; I tune my harp,
To sing the praises of our chief;
And set my teeth to eat roast beef:
Those who are gathered here today,
Are lingering in the shadows gray,
That mark the close of well spent life,
Filled with accomplishment and strife,
To win from Nature secrets rare,
Laws of the earth and sea and air.
We've seen our planet circled round,
With glowing light; and heard the sound
Of motors driven everywhere,
Their hum pulsating on the air;
And we've the joy of that blessed one
To whom the Master said "Well done".

YOUR TURN!

If you have visited more than one museum, then you might know that they can come in different sizes. Some are giant and sprawling. Others are in old, historic homes. And sometimes they are just the size of one room! What they all have in common is that they display artifacts that somehow relate to history, science, art, or culture.

The Lewis Latimer House Museum is no exception. It is in a building that was once Lewis Latimer's house in Flushing, New York. In it, you can find an exhibit on his life.

The Lewis Latimer House Musuem

WHAT DO YOU WANT TO SEE IN THE LATIMER MUSEUM?

Now that you've read all about him, what sort of things would you expect to find in the Lewis Latimer House Museum?

- What might you hope to find from his childhood?
- What about from his Civil War days?
- What might you find from his work as a draftsman?
- What about his inventions? Art? Music? Poetry?
- How important do you think it is to be able to see objects from history?

Now imagine that you grow up to be an inventor like Lewis Latimer, and in the future there is a museum that is all about YOU. And in this museum you find the following exhibits:

A series of enlarged photographs showing the people and places that were important in your life. **Who or what are they, and why?**

A glass cabinet filled with objects that are meaningful to you. **What are they? Why are they special to you?**

A small room that plays a film on your life. **What is it like? How long is it?**

A small theater featuring a short play about you creating your invention. **What is it? How did you make it?**

A tabletop displaying instruments or tools you used in your lab or office. **What are they?**

And finally:

The gift shop sells a book about your life. **What is the title of your biography?**

Let your imagination fly!

GLOSSARY

abolish (uh-BAH-lish) to put an end to something officially

abolitionist (ab-uh-LISH-uh-nist) a person who works to abolish slavery

activist (AK-tuh-vist) a person who supports a cause and believes in taking action to change things in politics or society

apparatus (ap-uh-RAT-uhs) a piece of equipment or a machine needed to do a job or experiment

carbon (KAHR-buhn) a chemical element found in coal and diamonds and in all plants and animals

carbonized (KAHR-buh-nizd) converted into carbon or charcoal, typically by heating or burning

citizens (SIT-i-zuhnz) people who have the full rights and protection of a particular country, such as a right to live there, to work there, and to vote in the country's elections

Confederacy (kuhn-FED-ur-uh-see) the group of eleven Southern states that declared independence from the rest of the United States just before the American Civil War; also called the Confederate States of America

Confederate (kuhn-FED-ur-it) of or having to do with the Confederacy of the American Civil War

defended (di-FEND-id) gave reasons for something, or in support of someone

discrimination (dis-krim-i-NAY-shuhn) prejudice or unfair behavior toward others based on differences in such things as age, race, or gender

drafting (DRAF-ting) composing preliminary drawings that visually communicate how something functions or is constructed

electrical engineering (i-LEK-tri-kuhl en-juh-NEER-ing) designing and building items that deal with the use of electricity

electricity (i-lek-TRIS-i-tee) a form of energy that is generated in special large facilities and carried through wires to other areas

enslaved (en-SLAYVD) unfair condition of being owned by another person

expanding (ik-SPAND-ing) becoming larger in size, range, or amount

filament (FIL-uh-muhnt) a fine wire or thread in a light bulb that glows and produces light

fort (FORT) a structure where soldiers live that is built to survive enemy attacks

immigrants (IM-i-gruhnts) people who move from one country to another and settle there

incandescent (in-kuhn-DES-uhnt) glowing with light as a result of being heated

obituary (oh-BI-choo-wair-ee) a notice of a person's death (as in a newspaper)

patent (PAT-uhnt) a legal document giving the inventor of an item the sole rights to manufacture or sell it for a certain period of time

plantation (plan-TAY-shuhn) a large farm found in warm climates where crops such as coffee, rubber, and cotton are grown

rival (RYE-vuhl) a person who competes with another person to defeat or be more successful than that person

secede (si-SEED) to formally withdraw from a group or an organization, often to form another organization

slavery (SLAY-vur-ee) unfair condition in which one human being is owned by another

witness (WIT-nis) a person who signs an official paper to prove that they were present when a contract, will, or other legal document was signed

INDEX

FURTHER READING

Claybourne, Anna. *I Can Be an Awesome Inventor: Fun STEM Activities for Kids.* New York: Dover Publications, 2019.

Tegtmeyer, Anthony. *Real Engineering Experiments: 25+ Exciting STEAM Activities for Kids.* California: Rockridge Press, 2021.

Tofel-Grehl, Colby, PhD. *Awesome Electronic Projects for Kids: 20 STEAM Projects to Design and Build.* California: Rockridge Press, 2021.

Zoehfeld, Kathleen Weidner. *Light Bulb: Eureka! The Biography of an Idea.* New York: Astra Publishing House, 2021.

Read the other books in this series:

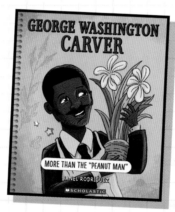

ABOUT THE AUTHOR

Janel Rodríguez is a "Nuyorican," that is, a Puerto Rican who was born and raised in New York City. She wrote the book *Super SHEroes of History: Civil Rights* for Scholastic. Like Lewis Latimer, she is a writer and an artist. She especially likes drawing people. The next time she has some free time, she plans on painting a portrait of Latimer himself!

ABOUT THE ILLUSTRATOR

As a child, Subi Bosa drew pictures all the time, in every room of the house—sometimes even on the walls! His mother always told everyone, "He knew how to draw before he could properly hold a pencil." Today, Subi continues to draw fun picture books, comics, and graphic novels from his home in Cape Town, a city in South Africa. He has won many awards for his work!